The Desert
Brandon Shimoda

The Song Cave

The Song Cave
Published by The Song Cave
www.the-song-cave.com

© Brandon Shimoda, 2018

Cover image: *Harvest Festival at the Tule Lake Concentration Camp*, October 31, 1942, by Francis Stewart. See note on page 177.

Design and layout by Janet Evans-Scanlon

All rights reserved. Printed in the United States of America.
No part of this book may be used or reproduced in any manner whatsoever without written permission except in the case of brief quotations embodied in critical articles and reviews. Members of educational institutions and organizations wishing to photocopy any of the work for classroom use, or authors and publishers who would like to obtain permission for any material in the work, should contact the publisher.

ISBN 978-0-9988290-6-7
Library of Congress Control Number: 2018947279

FIRST EDITION

Tucson, Arizona
2011–2014

Riding in a van through the desert, a former kindergarten teacher told us a story about a Pakistani woman who was murdered in East Tucson: the woman was murdered in her house. The woman's mother suspected the husband. She told her friends, but kept her suspicion private from her daughter's husband. She lost a daughter. He lost a wife. He didn't kill her. He was a doctor in Pakistan, but took a job in Tucson as a telemarketer. He and his wife had three children, a son and two daughters. The six of them, including the mother-in-law, lived in the house where the woman was murdered. The daughters were young. The son was mentally ill and had recently been institutionalized. Shortly after being released from the hospital and returning home, the son stabbed his mother to death. His sisters were in the house, but didn't hear anything. They were in the other room.

As I listened to the woman's story, we passed a tree farm. The trees were dark green in perfect rows. A cloud of dust whirled up from some kind of slovenly machine. I didn't know what kind of trees they were—pecan, maybe. I couldn't see any nuts from where we were on the highway, but the dark trees, the long, diminishing rows, and the whirling cloud of dust. I envisioned fetuses, pendant-like, enclosed in the womb of the trees. I thought of the daughters—were they twins? Did they hear their mother being stabbed? What were they doing in *the other room*?

The former kindergarten teacher said she taught both of the daughters—years ago (they're at the university now). She taught kindergarten for 35 years, had just retired (two weeks earlier), and was on her way to Hawaii to visit her daughter and grandchildren, who lived near Pearl Harbor. When I asked her what Pearl Harbor was like, she said, *There's still oil in the water.*

All I have done is incorporate the desert and the inconsolable into my displaced body. They have split me in two.

Malika Mokeddem

He said: I won't go to the desert
I said: Neither will I
Then I looked toward the wind /

Mahmoud Darwish

STREETS

The man says can you help me?
And I say can I help you?
It makes me angry he is happy
I am at peace he says
I am at peace
Yes I say
No I cannot help you
The difference between the man and me
I say to the man the difference between you and me
I am not asking if you can help me
I am not at peace I am not happy

INCARCERATION

There has to be a landscape
For wandering in place
For the nomad never leaves
The confines of the mind

Night. Siren sounds. A body is suffering
At the far end of the siren sounds
Close,

Leaping through the shadow
Pushing smoke through
The motherly
Spasm
Of the criminalized body
Sees? The criminalized body
In the traumatized season. The motherly spasm
Watching
The decimation   Impregnable,

The criminalized body becoming an implement
To divine the pulse of violation
In-progress   incomplete

Spasms multiply in the shadows
The criminalized body around the edge of light
                    the stars are dry
Feet are reptiles on the shingles
Blood on cactus is not murder
Yellow house is dirt
Caged in by a cyclone

The bashful branches of the river
First thing in the morning   the criminalized body
Slipped through

The sun
Could not color

Women with dentures
Bullfrogs in the overgrown canal
Running below
The face of the prison

Flowing 300 feet beneath   absorbed by the pigment
Flowing 300 feet beneath 150 women
Halation of unleavened heart works

Perpetual rejection is comfort
Conversation
In being rejected
Revealing, over time, divisions

Sheer   Yet temporary   Bodies
Suspended over the landscape   Crosses at night
Appeal from a distance
To the rejects   to be growing
Hearts   Neither sweats
Nor glows hungry
For what is advertised   resurrected whole hospice
Into a tighter soul market

MUSHROOMS

Asian American women
Appear to me in dreams

Mushrooms
Or rather women
Wearing mushrooms

I am standing in a house overlooking the sea
The house is on stilts, but short
The bluff is tall with cloudy grass
The sea is soundless, white
There is nothing in the house
There are windows, a doorway, no door

I watch a group of Asian American women walk up the bluff
Enormous mushrooms on their heads
The mushrooms look handmade
Flat-topped or bowl-shaped, Brandon, are you home?
This isn't my house, what sea is this?
The water is white. It looks hot

The women form a circle in the grass. I stand in the doorway
The women sit down. The circle becomes mushrooms
Shy and embarrassed. I want to join them

I recognize my hands outlined in black
On both sides of the doorway
Left hand on the right, right hand on the left
To reclaim my hands, I must resist interrogation
What are you? I am...
Sorry. We do not have one

The sea is apocryphal
White enamel
Floating surfactant over the bluff

The sun is eclipsed. It is day. I could go, but

The Asian American women are inviting me

I cross my arms before the doorway. I want to jump through the doorway
But I have candy   The sea has several

Why do I feel shy and embarrassed?

Returned like a parcel, told
GO TO YOUR HUSBAND
GO TO HIS FOOT

When I was young, I wore a fox mask
I took it off, and smashed it
Against a rock

When the sound was right
I wore it beneath

The sea does not encourage me. The sea is ugly
The high, white tide
Stings the shore

HOLY WEEK

Paper flowers
Beat against
The pediment of a church

Seed heads penetrate
The wind like
Flood

Flowers overhearing

Singing

Beneath NO REPRODUCTION

ONE FACE
Gentile profusion

Clown face with deer head
Deer head with braided faucet hair
                        garbage dust

Moth cocoons around ankles, deer hooves around waists

Masks remind us: independence is

To be mourned as much as celebrated
 loaves, fried hands and skull feathers
Shrunken vixen faces   starlet faces
Black diamond heads and carpet beards
Huntsmen faces   eagle faces

HOLY WEEK

I thought I was looking at a man
Walking across the street
Beneath the sky
Into a tree

I am looking at a man
Walking across the street
Beneath the sky
Into a tree

A momentary rush like
Two rushes in formation

The man presses his forehead into the trunk of the tree
Lifts off the ground, tries not to be awkward

The tree is green, limited
By the thought or so seems
Limited by the thought

That man has done THIS SHIT
BEFORE I have been sitting here, not abandoned, I would say
I have been walking HOT

And EARLY temperatures have begun
To put the puzzle in my mouth
Learning not what but HOW is melting

I'd watch such interactions turn to fable, simple
Changes conserved myself from
Work for this opportunity

Every morning I walk
To find the distance between
Images waking the common life
Forms alien in the sun

Wherever thought begins
Fighting
Calm, going
Forward from

Feels unfairly born, it's not, not
True, it never happened
That way origins of the world
Ripen, separate

To spare wanting to love
Everyone and everything because
What else, I mean really

When I've opened the field of view has
Come to me, or I to it
Beginning to recognize
That man, is he going to wake
Sore inside that tree, carrying what he's going to eat inside?
There is a slash of ants
Carrying cereal into the emerald

CHIMES

In the empty yard
CHIMES

Wind rinsing the fence
Rice cereal growing in the tree
Sea shells thousands of miles from the sea
A lantern perforated with stars

Virgin in the neighborhood
Ticking in the cactus
Solar lanterns floating

Before the caves

Virgin out of fashion
With real life   represents
Not in what real life is made
Real, I know   Virgin is there
Every night before the caves

REAL ESTATE   REAL LIFE
In bus shelters

Widows, widowers, burning (from) the shelter down

To be quenched, to be expelled
Before they can trust

Hands on

A shirtless man with white hair

Four-way intersections without Stop
The giddiness of Napoleon

Reaching for an infant
Held over the side of a boat

Worms entering or exiting
Menopausal women in the desert

Widows who dye their hair purple

Insects three feet off the ground

A man in a wheelchair
With a rectangle
Tattooed on his forehead

A broom with red bristles

Shadows of the star-perforated lantern

THE HORSE

A horse went walking in the river once
And fell into a hole
To its neck. The horse got stuck
People came around. Some people came around
And some people came around
And approached the horse
The people who approached the horse
Were at a loss. They could not extricate the horse
From the hole. They tried
To remove the earth
But only succeeded
In dropping

The horse was not wounded, however
All attempts to free the horse failed

The horse's neck and head were free
The horse could move its head
And breathe, and eat
So people brought it food—bags of carrots, apples
Grass from right there in the river

The horse was especially enthusiastic about lemons
Yellow godmothers. The horse's eyes blushed
Yellow godmothers. The horse's eyes squealed inwardly

The horse becomes in statue form
Four faceless, inanimate people
Embracing in the form of once-was-horse
Torn into additional
Expectorations

A field of carnivorous grass
Comporting an emerald kingdom

Figures are not FULL OF LIFE

Figures are quarantined
By fear
And make of love
A coping
Mechanism

Climbing, I am shredding

Fermented milk
Around the horse's gnawing mouth

I was, while urinating on a bank of snow
Against a deli, asking myself, what is it
I'm supposed to do? What is it I'm returning to?
My friends were passions in the parking lot
Twisting beneath, I remember

My shadow
Turning into the wall. Will I know enough?
To know I've left?
Enough?

To return?

To the lowest point?

The dissolution of the primal screw
Or chew the Gatorade
The horse loves, hangs its head over the fence
Am I supposed to touch? Enough
To see the yellow godmothers in the horse's eyes
Emblazoned with black Christmas trees

Fruit is blind. Only the tree sees
—René Char

What is the horse
That keeps on giving
Horse?

There's an old man in the river
Bringing food
On a tray
To feed the horse

The old man falls. The laughs pull off

People never outgrow
The desire to be
A hat upon the head
Of a body that cannot move

The basic obscurity
Of an animal in a field
Unknown because of speed

Talking to persons who are not there
The dirty horse is the journal
Of the absent persons' mental
Riding the horse, believing a voice
Satisfaction of the waste

A woman rides a horse into the desert
To make a portrait of herself
In the desert   with a horse, her horse
She will BE the desert, FROM the desert
As if she lives there, and has always

The portrait will be: THE DESERT
UNDERSTANDS ME

The desert
And I
Provide

The background is mostly sky. The ground tilts up
Where the ground meets the sky, the balance of the woman's body is
Not in it, the portrait: a horse, a dog, a river
Brush in the river, cactus in the river
Stars, the sky, crosses on a chapel
Small, insignificant flowers
Growing in the shadows of each
Cross imbuing with silent color
A critical double-portrait

MY ARTWORK COMES OUT
BETTER WHEN I MAKE IT
IN THE RIVER WITH
MY HORSE

What is the point? Hey you, ruining the view

Of fertile essences

When the desert is gone
All around is one
Way to regard it
Never was?

MOUNTAINS

There are the mountains, I see them
From town, the mountains are magnificent
Federal Bureau of Investigation, et cetera
Enormous the mountains are golden and black
When we go to the mountains, town becomes pathetic
But we miss it, we want to get back to the lights
We miss them, the lights, being thrown momentarily

From far away
The mountains several continents over
Three-quarters of the way
To access

Japanese Americans

∞ grandchildren
Who have been
Or who have never been
But someday
May
Or may not
Or may or may not want
To go to
Japan.   houses
By the emptied harbor
In the mountains   They will not enter
Will disappear from

Strangers who are familiar   are synonymous
Faces, outfits, interpreting attitudes
Withdraw into the burnt   The specter of a great-great-grandparent's
feet For example, being washed

Then the corpse
Relieves itself

Of having to be told, it is an assumption
That there is somewhere to be
Going, coming from

Like there are plants in southern Arizona
That, when stepped on, release an odor
Like a shadow that
Reforms a hood
That comes down just below
The nose

Behavior is adherence (to behave is to adhere)
To adhere is to be understandable
Not understood, to underlie the indoctrinating shadow of understanding
To cut your braid and hang it on the fence
Before the cave
Where the virgin makes
A show of praying

Hands are orthopedic. A thousand primitive white churches
Do not believe
In the immortality of the soul
Hellfire, predestination, the fleshly return of Jesus

Burning up the world. No hypostasis. Jehovah is a vocalization
The testimony of the conscience, conscientious objectors, resurrecting
Tabernacles in the pines
Temporary dwellings like camps

There was a prison labor camp in the mountains
The camp closed in 1973. The foundation is (tennis court is) still there

Labor equals the transplantation of war conscription
To public works, the benefits are the same

Eating chocolate chip cookies at the end of a road
Blazed by prison labor, rage
Private and public examples, passive resistance

The chocolate chip cookie
May or may not
Seem arbitrary
Even when it is being served   It is the grail
That lubricates a tourist
In the opaque eye of prison labor

The road it took
To achieve the chocolate chip cookie
Oversized   By it I mean the people
Who profit from the war
Inherent
In those who refuse
To let even placebo ordnance galvanize

Any margin of scenery in the future   Was built by Japanese Americans
Yamauchi, Norikane, Yoshida, Takeuchi, Yoshikawa,
Taguma, Kuromiya, Hoshizaki, Yenokida, Hirabayashi,
Hopi, Jehovah's Witnesses, Mexican Americans, African Americans,
Dissidents, conscientious objectors   Refractory,
They were called
To the chimeric intestine
Impaled upon the jagged ridge of
The magnificent mountain (plural)

The valley sinks
And everything we see, stinks to the roots
Transforming distance
Into a bedrock quality   far from action, where arms are, where
The road goes   Labor was imposed   was secret

No fence, no guard tower, but terrain erasing
The world, where the crests of the mountain meet the sky

Folds
The mind and the soul in

To the panoramic grave—

MONSOON

Because I thought we were going to die
By "die" I mean
Be
Momentarily transfigured
By falling
Into a racing depiction of our bodies

The medium-heavy mindlessness of living
As we do

In a monsoon,

Winds lash the house. The house bends. The alley fills with water
Trees bend in the skylight. A bird bends in the skylight
Coming over? Ruthless
Sensitivity
Makes us
Descendants
Of the first man, bloated corpse now
Plugging up
The once destitute wish made real

To die intervenes the commonplace
Ready to go out, sure
We looked like how we thought
And hours passed. There was a boat
To take us across the chocolate-colored river

In the mountain

The sun was lifting snow off the ground

Then I was in a small room with a cement floor
There was a drain, a dozen men in a circle

100%

Ashes now

To hate is to want the rib back

To infuse the imperial specter

For once, the territory relapses
While children eat bread
Baked in the gullet of an invalid god

To be above the unbearable stench of garbage
The stench is inclusive

Monsoon is soft romance
Boarding the body of the first man
Rowing down the alley

Sail like straws over roofs
And penetrate, by chance, the shelter of a creature
Coming to terms with the boundaries of itself
By what it can enter
And when
Darker areas start to move

Holding someone's arm
Thrusting it into the reflections of faces

People are snakes
Swimming only
To keep moving

BLIND CHILDREN

What is the raw fish popular in Japan?
Hawaiian bread
Instant memory
Hawaiian bread yes
Hawaiian bread tastes
Superior to
Those who are blind
Remember the taste
Before eating   Taste is prescience
Out-of-time
Hawaiian bread in schools
Blind children in schools

Fish are becoming women
In Japan
Killing whales
Japan's education system teaches children
It is OK to kill whales
Lesson #1
Blubber make-up
For the new piscine women
Swimming in lightless angel

Will never come around   They'll never get it
Around their eyes
Hungry with memory
For what is raw
And popular, popularly raw
In which case, Hawaiian bread
Has all the oceanic earth
Within it
Is the touch

BLIND CHILDREN

What is the first thing you remember?
Kicking my sister
My father hitting me with sticks
Lying next to my mother
Being hit, I can feel it
When I remember
Mother saying, But he's a miracle, when
The doctor said, He has 48 hours

BLIND CHILDREN

When Armando was eleven months old, he went for a drive with his father
It's the first thing Armando remembers:
Going for a drive with his father (being in the car with his father)
Facing backwards in his car seat

That is when his eyes opened

They were going to visit Grandma. Grandma lived somewhere (all around)

The second thing Armando remembers
Is his father resting his head against the window
He remembers his father resting
His head slowly
Against the window
Then his father's head against the window
As if his father was falling
Asleep. Maybe that is what Armando thought (that his father had fallen asleep)

The car wasn't moving (all around was not moving)

Armando's eyes were open. It was the last time he could see
It was the last thing he saw
His father looking
Like he was falling
Asleep against the window

Armando was trapped
In his car seat for two days. His father, not moving, asleep
Did not wake up, no sound
Came out, he dissolved. Armando could not see the road

The sky, small brown stuffs
Sitting on top of tall greens

The sun was in the car. Armando's skin was burning
The sun was not in the car. His skin was cool. His eyes were open
The whole time (burning, then cool)

When Armando closed his eyes, his eyes were open

He cried. He cried for two days
He did not fall asleep (Maybe he fell asleep)

Even after his uncle's voice was loud, and the loudness
Beat against the window (the window rattled)
Armando could not see the window
Bend. He could not see the glass
On his father's shoulder

He cried for two days. The two days did not end

Every reversing shadow became, still is becoming
A shadow reversing, still coming
To shatter the window

TRANSIT CENTER

The disorder of our feelings
Towards the order of our hearts
The disorder of our hearts, smoking on the box
Watching hearts dishevel and fall off the box
Into the arid sewer   to make the arid sewer run
With venom from the clocks
Screeching in the morning against the walls
With no one left, no one with nobody left
To plug them up, to turn them off

Man with man-eater, hula-hooping
For three young women
In black

Is
Master of ceremonies   Neck-dancing
In everyone's daydreams
MUSIC, GASOLINE

Miracle is burning

The officious hand of rancid air, grinding
Liberated souls
Into less expressive fashion

WE START ALL OVER, WHEN
WE ALL START OVER, become
Auxiliary
As when we were shot
Through anesthetic light
And brought to life
Within the sentence of existence

Fucking was an image
Of perfection   hanging on
The wall above a mattress

To be a bridge between the animal and the alien, the supernal spark
Must be arrested and chastised, the whole of heaven must be
Arrested and chastised
To a single tooth of coal
Burned down to
The arid sewer

The alien is even more animal than the animal
Our parents are the sleeping beauty
The first time our parents had sex, they fainted: two sleeping beauties

Fanning out above their bodies, toxic shadows

Country-lustful children
Toddling through blood
And feathers, archipelagoes of meat
Salty kneecaps, pools of skin

About the children?

There is a horse chained to the window
It can see 360° 100 miles into the distance
That is why the horse has fear
That is why the horse resembles ancestors in the sea

Elderly women with white heads and squirrelfish bosom
Elderly men with pink squirrelfish heads
Guns with pink heads

Animals know why the sky turns green
They hear a stampede, manure strafing
Purple desert before rain
After the fount of corpses
Humps up in the river
Boats untied, horses drowning
The man who plays piano
On the air   with many waters
ARK OF GARBAGE   A woman climbs into
The river, to press her face into a footprint

Watered religiously
And watched grow
The first legitimate sky
Reflected in a silver planet
Burning along the edges
Where nakedness is rejected

Before going out, kiss the mirror
Kiss the virgin, kiss the cross
Kiss the hole punched through the wall
Where a small plastic candle weeps into a DVD
Remember the tree? How it looked against the sky
After it rained? When you are older, you will see
Nothing is yours—not what you take, what you are given
Not how you change, what you have taken

Remember the bridge Grandfather built
Over the house, over the roof of the house?

We used to run up the bridge and pretend
We were old women running away
From the village on fire. We set the village on fire
The village was a giant awakening
Oceanic spirit of the desert

Disfigured into sun-eroded bodies
Running away from all our friends
Because we were all of them PERCENTAGES

We used to ask each other, if we were to set one building on fire
Based on how it would smell while it was burning
Which building would it be?
We both agreed—animals and food smell good at first
But go bad fast. Gas stations strip the veneer off the skull
Turn the sky into glass. Fire joins aborted fire in museums and books
Nocturnal, Pope tiptoeing on a string

Jesus appears in the middle of a ghost
Sleeps with an effigy between his knees
Snoring incontinent dogs upon the carpet
Buildings are fat, hairy legs
Swish hair is a mangrove

People in restaurants melt into their food
Animals drive hard and lick the plates
Reconstitute people as pre-human protoplasm
People born missing, stapled to fences, spray-painted on walls
Heroic in their lack of fruition

The herb shop would cure the festering harm
And harassment, all the misogyny
Misandry can stay. Misandry can fortify the remains

If we were to set the ceilings on fire
It would engender the sensation of falling up
To greet the saint
With a beatific smile

If we were to set fire
To successive layers of low atmosphere
Kites would spin into rays
And go ravenous over shadows cast
Across the coolly desperate pleas
Wrapping around the naked limbs
And charm-like adornments of
Premature corpsification

When two white people have sex that is incest
When two white people finish having sex that is dementia

The betrayal is ADULT

The corpulent magnet still hums
In the center of the heart, withers old men

Make a circle. Drop their pants. Dry river is louder
The drain in the center of the floor is most like it

The saint walks alongside bodies burning
To proliferate the smell of the burn
In a silent report, the saint has drums
On her mind   beneath the streets, colorless sprouts

Ghosts hate salt. Old women become children again
Lives of angels do not change
Stay amorphous as you were
Before determination

consciousness
…
occluded by
desire
desire for the
future
fruition
of the hour
and its
subsequent murder
…
…
no
attachment to it
…
we're all sitting
in a circle
…
…
to think
we won't all disappear
That is when I
piped up
…
I fell asleep on a rock
…
…
shamans prioritize
sleep, a
rich sleep

No, the stations of
the cross
suns
and flowers
growing in the suns

attempts at understanding
the incarnations of surveillance
understanding is the incarnation
~~skin is~~ skin
understanding
is becoming
the thing in the skin
the hearing child
the deaf parents
the child like a bar of soap
leprous parents
...
...
becoming sworn
to ritualize awe
...
...
...

...
...
...

There. I was traveling
Through the Alps
To get to the moon
I had to be Heidi
And sleep with the cows
All my parents were there, encouraging

The drunk couple
melting
into the street
Believe me
he says, We have to go!
She doesn't believe him
She's holding a bottle

A man wrapped in a wool blanket
eating a bear claw
at the gas station
…
The bear claw
falling
apart
…
The man's face
registers explosions
he's seen

at night
crustaceans come out

Are you from Tijuana,
the woman asks me
She's wearing a denim dress
and holding onto a walker

...

I can smell the stained glass
Her head is a house
Her body is legs

...

silver bells

...

No, I say, why do you ask
Because of your hat
It says TIJUANA
My hat says TAIWAN

A college student asked me if I was from Hawaii
No, I said, why do you ask
Because of your hat
It says Hawaii
A homeless man asked me
what my hat says
Does it say TAI-WOW

...

It says Taiwan
You been to Taiwan?
I go every summer
Every summer, what for?
I teach writing to children
crossing a huge intersection

Because it rained
All the cat urine is coming out
Because it has not rained
...
...
Two cats on a mattress   A mattress in the alley
Disappeared into the cubby
Every intravenous
Movement is a liability

Cats in a hole   small lives mostly
Obscured by a wall   but the hole
Permits a view

There's a luggage filled
with field guides
to tropical plants
and Mennonite children
...

...

...

inscrutable heads like: you will mix with
every other creation
but

It's where a man killed his wife
and kids then killed himself   ate his toothpaste
brushed with the dead wife's hairbrush

My uncle had a girlfriend
Until my aunt saw her holding hands with some other guy
and called my uncle
who called his girlfriend
and asked her where she was

...

she didn't lie
she said I'm through
come get your car
she left in the Walmart parking lot

...

He took the bus
and got his car
and hit a pedestrian
and drove away
but the cops caught up
and he went to jail
the pedestrian was OKAY
the pedestrian became a chaplain

The true expression of
one's dependency
on being men
terrible men
and aggressive
…
…
and autonomous women
thoughtfully combining
styles with a need
…
…
one dashing, refractory color

you shave one another
and hate and stand by one another

Running from the flames
The town was burning
like a giant
reawakening
the oceanic spirit
of the desert
disfigured
into
sun-eroded bodies

The pope softens
sensuality to a greeting
and as I'm reading,
the letters change

My face cracked
Lips ~~broke~~ were hiding behind a beak

I'm in bed w/the door open
...

Pink clouds   Green bushes
Nerve endings   Black bushes
Green   a sphinx-like home
~~The green~~   ...
...   ...

Lemons in a small tree
...

a hole in the floor
Darkening pink
...

A middle-aged woman with
    broomstick legs
...

She loves ornamental vegetation
To be authentic, pure
dog is more comely
...

As it turns out
The hole radiates
A little funnily
Before falling through the floor
...
...

I open the door
...

Black bushes
Clouds
I ate an eye
~~And~~ tossed in bed
Then

There's a bag of manure in the alley
By the enormous garbage   smells like manure
And a black lizard   Two grasshoppers
Killed a moth
...

...

A woman coughs twice
...

...

We don't have deer, but there are people in the alleyway
looking for food... cans or clothes
can mate anything

My friends were good
and they were there
where I was
~~watching them~~
admiring them,

...

then the clock stalled
the air stagnated
into a pantomime

...

...

My friends ~~was~~ were friend
spoke comically abt death
How we're all missiles, etc.

...

But I remember the music
I would not have known
Because I'm still listening
The music has aged

The girl reads beneath a tree
The girl's face is incomplete
but has a mother, which doesn't mean her
mother completes her
…
Dark book with
Gregorian sentences

a flower in which
she nevertheless
sees herself
…
her voice
in the soundlessness
of her parents'
…
reverberations

The ornament
is not the tree's preaching
satellite
burning out
…
to a mirrored rock
in which evolution
…
is reshaped

Everything has become
instructional
…
…
…
messengers of gravity
…
children
…
do not instruct you
blind thru the
corridor w/out walls

the arid lime
of a savior squatting
over an unkempt shadow on the ground

Does not that diminish
exercises?

A pink crow
placed upon
the wall
...
is white,

Or you make peace
you cordon off

To envision with clothes
To see with clothes
…
…
Hot contours on a wall
To be restored
And want to mount it Climb on top
As if communion
Climbing in (it)
Naked cross
The smell of mollusks in August

every / every poem
written to the person
I was becoming
before I became
the person writing
every poem
over and over again,
    my bridge, my love

become a person   in between
you did not know   recognizing
you were   evaporating
because they said so   into the displacement
became another, third   remains
voice of the terror   you have chosen

Where you can't be
in maps
…
as with your thoughts
…
…
not even where is being
…
…
in the formless territory
that roars before you
home is a deception
…
in the cracks
that hold the wall together →

I dream of the flood
that will bring the lake
in dreams immortality
…
it dreams immortality
…
in the black veins of
the house collapsed

I dream of the fire
that will illumine
…
the survivors
the sustainers
the famine
…
conceiving
…
…
where the vicious ore
capers a new luminosity
I see ~~the flood~~ waters
rising in the veins
of a new nation
I see fires in ~~arcing racing~~ in
long, razor
arcs
over the waters
DOLPHIN

existence is posthumous

THE HOODED BRIDE

She ~~will~~ won't be
A bride
If she follows through
If she follows
Herself
Through the mirror
...
Better to be nobody
...
...
...
...
Sensational   Foreign
Language in the season
...
Touches sound   without
The science of its cells (parts)
...
That loves suspension   ~~from for~~
The shadow (that)
~~Separates~~ Takes shape
~~W~~ In ~~the~~ momentary Separation
...
Solar (premonition)
Of the ancient body
Returning

Why is the mirror
Stone. I can't
See anything
In the mirror,
...
...
...
...
That's what it means to be
A citizen: <u>erasing</u>
...
Love. Because I love

I am suspect

You are
In your own
Imagination now   precisely
Where you will yourself, light breaks across
The hood   Light breaks across the hood
Light breaks over

Good. We can
Appreciate now
The cubic moonlight
Lowering over our bodies
Entangled in the weightless paste   Melodious pyramids
In the trees   Moonlight on dogs' faces
...
...
...

We could touch thru our eclosures stick our hands through
Speaker boxes
And dream of walking thru the trash, into
The ~~baking battleground~~
The dream satisfies
The desire
To live on the outside
Not in the nationless hall, the
Excoriating primer
Of the nation
Emblazoned

"LAST LOVING HOUSE"

The bride's flying (sailing) over
The "LAST LOVING HOUSE"

Warm plants on the fans
...
~~The bride passes~~   The bride's sailing over
...
Her shadow // the train
Sleep to the mewling
...
Inside the cedars
...
...
...
...
Lines that thicken
Censoring (redaction)
A mirror on the back of a neck, disembodied
Segment of robe (rainbow)

I am the sea I am the weed
Hair with eyes   Momentary corpse
That sees the sky   sends up the sky
In waves
...
...
The circle (maru)
Cuts through me,

Separated, I become

...

Together, re-form

...

...

The sea in the desert
The fossil on the floor   on the bed
~~Scoured by~~ Burnished by the sun
To a mirror

Carries through
In the bag   Smile on the wall

...

...

Mountains scored on the walls
Rinsed of gold

...

Melted into
Small, morning cups
By the rising and falling of the lake

...

In a ring
The world's remains

I wash my hands
On the bride's multifarious stone, down to
A single figure   A mollusk I make
Sails in through the
Dark, sails over

...

Nerve of the sun

...

...

Emanations

...

...

Ring in the earth
The sea circulates

...

Having ~~done~~ done their work
Having labored

...

...

Corpse light
~~The blue~~ Settles
The ~~ca~~ mouth of a cave
Black hair on a hooked bloom
And the facet of an eye

...

...

If she stops moving, she touches
The center of the circle

...

...

...

...

How much sun
Can you abide
Before you it burns
Through you _____

My heart is racing. First morning in Tucson. No sleep last night. No food since yesterday morning. Looking for garbage in the streets to make a new garbage book. Have I told you about my garbage books? Spiral-bound garbage, which I send to Phil. I wander the streets looking for garbage. It's how I re/acquaint myself. This morning, first thing I saw: a hawk standing on a pigeon corpse in the post office parking lot.

January 13

I woke up this morning in the desert. After eight months away. We were in Nova Scotia, and I had the feeling, the *sensation*, of writing to you about where we were, maybe I even did . . . because I was, anyway, talking volubly to myself, but the form disappeared, or was disappearing, into the landscape, a very established rock through and around which water was the changing population.

January 15

I am sitting in our friend's backyard. There are two birds. The orange tree is bare. Yesterday, DD and I went for a walk in the desert. I wondered aloud, *Do animals exercise?* Just then, we saw two deer on the hillside in front of us. They emerged from the cactus and rocks; two of them, parent and child. Something was gleaming: the parent had a silver arrow stuck in its neck. The parent did not look fazed, and there was no way to tell how long the silver arrow had been stuck in its neck, but instantly, the rest of the "world," the landscape, the people passing by on the path—we were sitting on a rock ledge—became the bearer of silver arrows.

January 17

It's hot again in the desert. People have taken the bed sheets off their bushes.

January 21

The desert is always good about erasing a good deal of the rest of the world. The oldest place, the youngest place, the only place . . . all else seems, from this vantage, like outdated machinery, screeching and screwing its way to a much-needed oblivion.

January 22

It has been a long time since I've lived anywhere with an accessible roof. Not since Mexico. There was a small garden on the roof, and a chair. I could inhale the rivers, and the bottoms, where the street dogs would go to die. I could see the lights from the flame trees. I had a terrible nightmare in that house, was crying and screaming so loud I woke the district. A woman ran a taco stand down the street that opened at 11 pm. There was a small black-and-white TV above the comal you could watch through the steam.

January 30

Sometimes, after the sun goes down, this apartment feels subterranean. The darkness presses at the windows for the sense of there being nothing outside; these neighborhoods don't have many, or any, street lights . . . Last night, biking home from the river, where John and I went to walk the dry river bed, we passed through neighborhoods without ANY lights, but the lights on our bikes, and the occasional light adorning a jogger, two little dogs. My night vision is horrendous; I become blind . . . as wonderful a feeling as it is terrifying.

January 31

Back in the public library. The woman sitting to my right just found out she has cancer. Ovarian. She's on the phone.

February 3

Did you touch St. Francis's face?

February 4

I was thinking, meanwhile, that defects, deformations, disease, where they do not merely manifest the folds, make additional folds, make visible the folds . . . and we can see, at last . . . direction, presence, omni-presence, omni-direction, become visible, that we can see, like the folds in painted scrolls, which are necessary and terrifying, the hinges.

The desert has dropped a few degrees today.

February 4

I've eaten very little today, though last night we biked to a Mexican restaurant exactly 34 blocks south of our apartment.

February 5

Is it night? I ate my clock . . . Now I'm in a small, windowless cubicle. The table is wood and sturdy, but faceless. Above me is a metal shelf. There are three books on it, all with green covers: Sawako Ariyoshi's *The Twilight Years*, Kobo Abe's *Ruined Map*, and *The Story of Yokohama*, a book for children. I have been in here most days, when not subbing or otherwise dragging the city . . . There is nothing, really, to STARE at. But the RHINE . . . What of it can you see? What does it look like today, or the last time you looked?

February 5

It's an exceptionally quiet day. You would like it here—the desert, this part of it, green, pale-green. The sense of space, or space's sense, how things alternate dimensions upon the eye, flattening out, no distance to perceive, then everything being distance, the crackling of red ants out of a hole, aloe plants browning and falling over, some column arising in the place of the vanquished heart.

February 6

This morning, I shook a kale leaf—hundreds of aphids fell off . . . Then I walked to the edge of the yard . . . and stood at the cement-block wall . . . I hung from the wall.

Then I came here: the public library. Someone urinated on a chair. So the librarian, a middle-aged man, turned the chair over. A couple days ago a bird flew into the glass door. The librarian was showing his vacation photos to someone. He went to Cambodia. Looking at one photo he said, *Look! I was skinny back then!*

February 13

Yesterday, DD and I went for a walk in the desert, just below the mountains to the northwest. A profusion of cactus. So many, of so many varieties. We came upon a sign that said, BEWARE: ACTIVE BEE COLONY. We stopped, and listened. We could hear bees—we could hear the SOUND coming from the cleft in a large rock. If we concentrated, if we had stayed, would the cleft have produced, in the form of bees, a buzzing cataract?

February 19

Drove by a sign today that said, El Rey del Elote. This was after eating fry bread with beans and cheese at San Xavier Mission. I needed a change of scenery, so we started driving. Straight south. Into the pecan trees. The people disappeared. The trees, bare . . . Roared up. As the dynamo. The milky way. At the end of the book. All books.

February 23

I am sitting in the house of a poet. She is out-of-town and DD and I are house-sitting . . . I can't write yet, or do anything, really, because I'm not familiar with this house, this space. There's a cat. Paintings on the walls.

Vegetation. A mountain to the north. And a lake nearby, which is rare for the desert. On the lake are coots, like black ducks . . . But I did have a premonition of what I will write when I'm ready, when the house is: when we walked out of the museum we were overcome by the scent of orange blossoms.

February 25

Everything outside is some incarnation of yellow or cream, which is desert and dust: the cream-colored folding chair, metal . . . my back against the yolk-yellow wall, the aloe plants yellowing—I broke one limb of an aloe with my foot, absent-mindedly, thin flowers with miniscule yellow petals, the sun on the white petals of the cane crossing the window is aging.

February 26

I have been listening to the neighbors' chickens. Some of the chickens are ducks. Some are asleep . . . It rained last night, which means the riverbeds, normally dry, are wet . . . not with river . . . but a sub-terrestrial expression of sky.

March 2

I spent the last hour raking the backyard. Weeding and raking. All rocks. Mesquite leaves and tumbleweed tendrils and mint-green weeds. I found two broken pigeon eggs. All gardens here are like Japanese karesansui, dry rock gardens, with the sun starting to go.

We're in a different neighborhood now. Less amenities, less of everything. More garbage, broken glass . . . Quieter. A little more desperate, everyone and everything baking to wafer-thin paralysis . . . The neighbors have a large grapefruit tree. They brought some grapefruits over the other day. Fat ones. Juicy.

March 10

The sun just rose over the roof of the house across the street and is now in the mesquite, basting the heads of the ceramic warriors on the sill, their arms around each other, their faces scored, scarified, orotund feathers hanging from their necks.

March 16

I did not see a rainbow today, but melon water on the mountain, and a 400 year-old pile of soil.

March 17

There's a small urn filled with a dead poet's ashes on the bookshelf, and I'm afraid of knocking it over. The ashes would fall upon a pillow, then the cat would lick them up, and I'd have to assemble a substitute from the dust . . . I watched a man yesterday in the dry riverbed running his brown horse through exercises, up and down the sand drift, then spent the rest of the day fantasizing about the horse's nostrils.

March 23

In addition to that horse, and the man riding it, I keep seeing this young woman in tight maroon pants descending into the dry riverbed. I've seen her three times. Each time she's entering the riverbed in the same spot. There is trash and mesquite trees and broken glass and waterlogged sleeping bags and creosote bushes, and the woman, gaunt, descending into the guts. The guts . . . are filled with the footprints of ghosts. Even after it rains, after the dry riverbeds flood, the footprints remain . . . Ghosts are always on the move. Then what does the woman do? She lays face-down in the riverbed and presses her nose into a footprint.

March 25

With that, a wind just picked up . . .

Still, a mourning dove is calling from the trees.

March 25

The bougainvillea is turned-on this morning, and the cactus is idiotic.

March 30

The bougainvillea is very hopeful . . . I can hear wooden shoes clopping down the street . . .

Beneath the prison is an extensive network of prairie dog tunnels.

March 30

The solar lights have just come on. Not even purple scores the sky. I haven't left the house today . . .

I got stung by a bee. A single drop of blood rose to the surface of my finger. I call that single drop of blood THE QUEEN.

I've been riding my bike up and down the dry riverbed, slaloming around . . . mounds of garbage, waterlogged sleeping bags. A homeless man was murdered in the river. Johanna saw his body being pulled out by the police. He was murdered by two other homeless men. His name was Owen.

April 1

I saw two rabbits yesterday. One living, one dead. One was hopping through a swale of garbage. The other was a cyclops, flat on the road.

April 1

Fresh off a day with blind teenagers. I'm beginning to understand our biological connection to atomic bombs and coelenterates.

April 2

There are pigeon eggs in the yard . . .

Some are broken . . .

The pigeons roost on the roof . . .

They start clamoring early in the morning, making noises like submarines . . . Sometimes I wave a broom around the backyard like I'm conducting lightning.

April 4

The cactus are charged with homogeneity.

April 4

I've been feeling less comfortable in crowds, even when the crowds are small. But music rights me. It doesn't eliminate the crowd . . . but brings the attic out of them . . . A head-strength. An anti-society. Like the wooden legs that adorn the ancient shrines. I've been staring at four black-and-white postcards of Toji Temple (Kyoto) Mary Ruefle gave me, trying to locate the bass . . . I hear young men with shaved heads chanting in a dark room, and feel the secret organization.

April 6

You asked me once, *Can you live in the desert?*

Do you remember asking that?

April 7

Strong, sonic winds . . . Brown flowers, folded, cupped, are tossing at the windows, the windows of our new, temporary space: a pool house three blocks from a Korean restaurant and a comedy club.

April 8

Peoples' heads hand-molded into primordial shapes, people walking without bending their knees, wearing see-through sweaters, riding on dogs, moving one frame at a time.

April 10

There's a humming in the neighborhood. The humming is white, translucent. Like a battery or a beehive. Maybe the correctional facility . . . I noticed the yellow blossoms on the paloverde. Young and yellow and resourceful.

April 10

I've been admiring the cactus, wondering about their age. I've been seeing the contours of refugees. Occasionally I see horses. Mostly homeless people. A homeless man was drawing in the sand with a stick. Another homeless man was drinking a 2-liter bottle of Dr. Pepper. I say hello to the prison every time we pass. And I've been spending time with blind children.

April 17

What an amazing trick of the sun: to appear so calm, steady, lethargic . . .

On this rock . . .

Because . . . do you know what the sun sounds like?

DD and I went to Reed Park with a blanket and a small stack of books and read poems by 13th c. Chinese concubines.

April 23

Yesterday I saw a pigeon that had been decapitated. It was under a bridge. When I went back underneath the bridge, there was another bird in its place . . . a baroque black bird, with a collar like an extravagant carnation.

April 23

We attended a Holy Week ceremony of men dressed in black gowns with black hoods and large men and small boys in wooden masks and wooden swords and a bonfire of black trash bags filled with trash and fry bread with beans and dust . . . Much of the ceremony was spent idling: nothing happening, things constantly on the verge . . . Then two large women started singing. A makeshift cloth canopy was held above their heads while they sang, people drank soda and I watched the festoons of paper flowers.

April 23

I've been floating in an airless state the past few days. How can I describe it? It found its nighttime twin in the bike ride DD and I took last night along the dry riverbed. We were being guided by my small, senile bike light, and the aura of light from a neighborhood. The mountain to our right looked bathed in moonlight, but there was no moon. We could only see a few feet in front of us. For all the lights I've just described, there was no light. The bike path was black. The black was engulfing. The engulfing was FILLED with RABBITS. Rabbits darting back and forth across the path, in and out of the creosote.

April 24

Sun beating down on a pile of bricks beneath a prickly pear cactus in (yellow) bloom.

April 27

Spent 2 hours this morning at City Court, attempting to appeal a $300 traffic violation. My license has been revoked the past month, got reinstated this morning, but would rather walk until my shoes fall off my feet, or I fall out of my shoes.

May 1

Today we rode our bicycles to the art museum to look at the Tomb Model of a Noble's Home (Eastern Han, AD 25-220), a clay three-story house, figures standing on the balcony, beatific smiles, looking out, and I thought: they're waiting for the dead . . . It's a homecoming. And I thought: what is something that is MADE by the living—by an individual—that yet PRECEDES the living—the individual. A dream? A tomb? A poem? When we make something and it seems, once *complete*, or integrated, in some way, that we are CATCHING UP TO IT.

May 6

Sitting here with both doors open, letting in the morning—two toddlers, boys, just wandered into the apartment—looking like carnival performers, dressed in overalls, with mullets, should have been wielding little mallets or with handle-bar mustaches—one boy had a broken piece of bread in his hand—neither old enough to speak. We just let them wander around . . . the poor genius of the morning.

May 8

Going on 3+ weeks without a night's sleep. Is it possible to fall in love with a dripping faucet? Also, a woodpecker was pecking on an electric transformer this morning, which was creating such an excellent sound, I dashed outside, and two mourning doves flushed from a bush knocked over a garbage can.

May 8

Night is a condition. A terminal condition? The sun is middle-aged. There's a woodpecker on the mesquite. The woodpecker is a consequence of the sun being middle-aged. Aren't we all?—storytelling by the fire.

May 13

We went to a Yaqui Holy Week ceremony in which all the men wore hand-carved masks, each fitting their personality, or the projection thereof . . . I felt like we were witnessing the inflation of individual psyches along the shores of the afterlife, which then cast me backwards and forwards (at once) into the utter marvel that is THE HUMAN FACE, unmasked.

May 15

Here are two sleeve dancers:

They have something in common with the cactus I've been spending time with . . . They seem to be incarnations (iterations?) of each other, in their effortless calculations, being mountain-inversions, or antennae, inward laughter.

May 20

There was a solar eclipse yesterday . . . People were gathered on the mountainsides staring at the sun through black lenses, tiny holes in cardboard—for once it felt like we were able to commune with our mutual source. Strangers were offering each other grapes.

May 21

I don't know what day it is anymore. It is 106. I slept for eleven minutes last night. My mind is a wandering atlas . . . I officiated a wedding this past weekend, in a small chapel surrounded by cholla with a full view of the mountains to the north. The sort of place where an old-fashioned dust-up might happen, blood and pieces of brain . . . the floor of the chapel light with flowers.

May 23

Sitting in the yard. Awaiting the bobcats, the nocturnal gremlins. Been seeing a lot of feral cats. Springtime? People too. Seem to be on the rise. Man belly-dancing at the bus depot. Wearing a belt of little bells. I've been in-and-out of consciousness. Was pretty low yesterday. Wandering aimless through the old neighborhood. Had to call DD to pick me up. Couldn't walk any further and couldn't find shade to take a nap. Drank some limeade and went to sleep. The tether keeps fraying. I console myself by taking notes on the desert, and its rightness for this state of being. Music and the well-timed seam through literature. Plus, the right dosage of alcohol before I become inappropriate and frighten my friends. Personal life largely withered? Backyard reading? How's Ginger? Have you found other music down the mean streets? Notes on scraps? Making messes in the garage? Turning on your guitar? Opening the rubber cement?

. . .

Back on the bicycle today. Fixed the brakes, rode into midnight. Shirtless man with pierced nipples walking the riverbed, muddy water (monsoon . . .)

August 2

But what I wanted to tell you is that there's a river in the (Santa Cruz) river, man, like fucking magic: roaring, rushing, brown, muddy, fecal, wilderness, beautiful. I wish you could see it. Surely you've seen it before. My first time. Like I was high. Bullfrogs emerged in the reeds. Fat, stentorian, belching, especially in the canal near the prison.

August 3

I took the prison route home last night: where the river splits, the prison sits like a vibrating battery. A short bridge spans a derelict canal, but because it's been raining, the canal is filled with bullfrogs . . . prisoners throwing voices.

August 3

It is night. I'm sitting in a very loud place. There are many young people here. I'm sitting across from DD. My head is splitting. I just ate a pile of seaweed . . . DD ate a pile of tofu. We are going to the movie theater soon, to watch a documentary . . . Earlier this evening, riding our bicycles around the empty streets of Tucson . . . we watched bolts of lightning burn through the sunset . . . over the mountains, veils of rain sweeping the peaks. Every day ends like this.

August 27

How goes the ghost world? How are things opening? Have you had any spirit encounters? Have you eaten any yellow cactus buds? Figs, there are fig trees on the university campus. But then, the campus might be gone (by now), replaced with a wave pool of exorbitant, indescribable color.

August 31

We met the nudist. She was a white woman . . . She said she'd been standing naked in the rain the night before, because it was rare, and she wanted to be penetrated . . . Her son is 48 and addicted to oxycontin. She said her mother was killed in an airplane crash, but it was okay, because her mother wanted to die. In fact, her mother KNEW the plane was going to crash. How did she know? *Our bodies are just vehicles,* she said. Then she said, *I hope this is my last vehicle.* To which I said, *Pretty strange vehicle.* She said she had a good feeling about us. She had an Irish accent, but when I asked about her ethnic background, she said, Romanian, Russian, and gypsy. Maybe that combination makes Irish. It was pouring rain when we left.

September 9

I am a cricket beneath the quietly lumbering clouds.

September 26

A cat was murdered by a coyote three days ago, it's body parts strewn about the park . . .

I heard it . . . thought it was a baby.

October 1

Moments after I wrote you that last email, I got sick. I walked out into the SUN, the SUN I had been speaking of, towards the library, when a feverish wave rose within me, and I came crashing down. I spent the last few days lying on a day bed, embroidered with spirit reindeer and mandalas.

October 2

Not sure why I keep prefacing every email with mention of *the desert*, though the affirmation feels necessary. This is where we are, this landscape which feels as congenital to our condition as it does alien. I still have little sense of what it is, what it does . . . We had a nice $3 meal at the Hare Krishna center in town.

October 3

I was talking yesterday to a man with no teeth about to get on the bus to see a movie at the $1.50 theater. He begged $$$ for bus and movie. He was going to beg $$$ to get back to where he started. This was on the sidewalk outside a coffee shop near our apartment. I was sitting outside, using Internet, to send my bank information to the HR department of the School for the Deaf and Blind, where I've just been hired as a substitute. The man was going to see a movie titled *Brave*.

October 3

I have only ever gotten lost. I am—even now, even still—completely inarticulate on the subject. Especially now considering ways of entering and/or re-entering. I take the desert to be my Lady of Solitude. I appeal to her. The desert is the landscape of coordinated disappearance. *Nationalism always requires an enemy, whether inside or outside the nation*, Angela Davis says. The vortexes of racism, oppression, profiling, incarceration, and silencing (silence) are widening so tremendously they no longer resemble such previously *rarefied* spaces, so that it has become redundant even to say that such histories are *relevant*, because of the fact that they HAVE NOT STOPPED / ARE NOT HISTORIES. The continuum is ongoing; the target is the soul.

October 3

Up with the clouds, 6:30, amazing cloud cover, moving thick, fast, occasional crowns bathed in the highest light, though the sun is nowhere, the birds are crazy with morning market . . .

DD's birthday's today. She's asleep. People coming over in a couple of hours. I asked everyone to bring records to play.

October 11

I was thinking about the apocalypse, not as some cataclysmic event, but as a slow revelation of the inside of existence, and what the hollowness revealed, which would be counter to what everyone expects, an out-pouring of the human history, geological history, magma, horsemen, disease, all the oceans at once, as though pulled through the navel of the world: just space, and ash, that we've arrived late, and the apocalypse is the revelation of what already took place.

October 19

Just now, biking back from the library, an ambulance drove over a book. Right before it drove over the book, it turned off its siren, but kept its whirling lights on. The book was CAUGHT, then grew like a moth.

October 21

There are clouds this morning, and it feels like a visitation. So far the days have seen feature-less skies, or a sky, feature-less—an enlivened yet spartan blue. A blue without space, irretrievable depth, except in the morning, when the sun pulls away. The mountains give depth, distance, but the sky is drugged, however beautiful, somewhat exotic . . . clouds! They are here, however slight. I hope they pull themselves further, the smell of rain in the desert is exciting, stirring up oils from the creosote.

October 24

Now I am self-conscious. I will landscape Siberias.

October 24

Every morning a little dumber to the fact that the appreciable grave is the space between my body and the floor, and as my body devours the shadow, if there is one. Most often there is none. Occasionally there are two, as like the moon last night, a perfect boat, jaundiced on the ancient peaks. I killed a moth last night thinking it was a cockroach (because our casita is a hive of cockroaches), and found it clinging this morning to the white bricks.

October 30

My memory of the other night is pedaling through the completely empty streets adjacent to the street the parade was on—thinking to myself how narrow the range of festivities . . . that it wasn't radiating out . . . but so respectable to the route. Then the image of the woman (?) twirling in white ribbons, suspended over the flames and dancing and gawking bird people on stilts and the masses like royal jelly purple. When the people lit the blinding flares, a beautiful vision was struck of the crowd gazing up in anticipation.

November 7

It rained this morning, which means floods. We climbed into the car for the first time in three weeks, and drove over the washes. We drove past a butte coarsely tufted with cactus and creosote, on top of which sat a cloud. We stopped into a bakery up north that was offering free breakfast; we cleared out their buffet and emptied both of their jugs of iced tea. Some of the most beautiful trees in Tucson are in the cemetery north of town. Most of the palm trees are in the trailer parks. The water disappears quickly.

November 13

It has been raining for twelve hours straight, which is a desert wonderment . . . not so much talking about *the weather*, but sharing with you a heaviness having settled upon the desert, if momentarily, where normally I feel lightness, even in its occasional embodiment of hell.

November 13

I was just sitting in a noisy bar, eating half a sandwich, alone . . . It has been raining for twelve hours, the streets are flooded. Walking back to here (I'm in the kitchen), was walking through the primordial possibilities, feeling like the desert has a very basic desire, a desire which is in fact everywhere present, only underneath the resolve of the world as it is, which is tiring to think about, but tiring to do anything, anywhere. We went for a drive through the desert this morning . . . passed a butte with cactus and creosote up its skirt . . . on top of the mountain sat a discus-shaped cloud, which seemed incapable of lifting off, or blowing away. I thought, it looks like white hair, but is it a halo? Is it a question gripping itself? Has it been punctured by the cactus on top, and therefore cannot move? The valley opened up on all sides, and still we drove through the rain.

November 13

I realized, again, that all of my writing is addressed to the dead, if not death itself. The apocalypse might necessarily be assumed, as with physical decay greeting a young body in the first quarter of its life, at least; to be born, etc. Narrative, song-making, meter, then into the lyric, ornament, guitar solos, orthotics: furnishing the eye of the storm, while drawing from its multipronged winds. We're either building our tombs or consoling ourselves by poking tiny holes in an enormous lead vest, to let a sample of light in, while the apocalypse presses with the fervor of 5000 fingers.

November 13

One of my favorite Japanese folk songs is for the Bon Odori (O Bon) dance in Hokkaido. My sister gave me the record. Seeing the dance, it does seem as though the women, the old women, especially, are never going to stop turning in their circle . . . I start envisioning them wearing a helical ramp down into the earth, where heaven is, not hell, very slowly the bridge between worlds.

November 13

But there is a point, a measurable point, at which the EYE and the STORM meet, and I think there is some form of responsibility in touching it. I am very sad that the street car is making progress. I would prefer to see the roads FOREVER TORN TO SHIT, because that seems far more honest than the BOTULISM being injected into the surface of things.

November 13

We recently moved to Tucson, on something of a lark, as all our decisions over the past seventeen months have been made using ouija and dart board. There is an observatory here, free in the evenings. The other night we stopped by and saw JUPITER, with its four moons, one of which is PURE WATER. I think that moon is called EUROPA, but now I'm not trusting myself. We were engulfed in the IDEA of storms that rage eternal.

We've been dog-sitting for our friends, who live next door—we're squatting in the studio above their garage, but are vacating on Saturday morning, getting on a Greyhound, Los Angeles. We sleep on a mattress the size of a splinter. I've fallen off twice . . . This morning I am pedaling to the Center for Creative Photography, on the university campus, to meet, for the first time, a photograph taken by my grandfather in the 1930s. They have one of my grandfather's photos in their collection!

DD is light and speed and vegetable. She's at home here, used to live here, so moves with a liberal grace. She's working on a screenplay with a friend, and is also writing a book about the Midwest (title: *MW*). She drinks a lot of stevia-sweetened soda, so I wrote to the company telling them this, and they sent us a box of twenty-four cans!

November 17

I was very nearly over over. I ate a tongue for dinner. The room was poorly lit, but warm, with the feeling of a blunt-edged eve. Large cup-like orange flowers were spilling out of a glass vase. The tongue came recommended, and was delicious. Now I am facing a doorway, and am dressed to go into the woods . . .

November 23

I had a dream:

DD was arrested . . . The charge? She had been using a fake mirror. She was caught using a mirror that reflected reality, not the reverse of reality.

November 24

Somehow your question, *Can you live in the desert*? feels relevant.

November 28

What if it isn't angels? What if the angels are not perfuming themselves away from/against the sharp edge of the second scissors? I just met this woman:

She was on a wall on my walk. There's nothing below this image. I mean: she's not holding anything, though it looks like that's where it's going. Then I saw a roadrunner. But first, there was another woman beside this woman. The latter was missing an eyeball. Men were on the roof. One of them said Hello. How are you? What have you been listening to? But then I thought: the roof. Maybe there are answers up there. Not the umbrellas, etc. who knows what they were doing. They were older men, neatly dressed.

November 28

A season, it seems, has come and gone. Or, in the parlance of the desert, here, come and coming. I was scolded for not acknowledging that the desert has not one, or two, or even four, but thirty-plus seasons.

Life here is slow, then busy, slow again, mostly good. I've been subbing at a school for the deaf & blind, which has me feeling a little deflated, like today, for example, each one of these words individually hand-drawn. Scattered across a variety of projects that seem to have neither start nor finish, save for a new book of poems, which is moving with the consideration of a snail across a banana leaf.

November 30

I don't know who the wolves are, or if there is only one, refracted. I spent today with three elementary school children—P (11), V (8), J (12). P, V, and J are low-functioning. Their class is called *Life Skills*. P has the cognitive development of a 9 month-old; V has cerebral palsy on one side of her body, her siblings don't speak to her, she spends all day playing a battery-operated keyboard; she wet herself three times today, so wore four different pairs of pants throughout the day; J was born without a nose, has under-developed eyeballs, and has the physical development of a 4 year-old. In another time and place, what would have happened to them? What is happening to them now? Sometimes I see them with perfect clarity, and I think they're seeing me.

November 30

What does enervation become? Is it permissible to wish the wind be even more relentless? DD and I have been absolutely rapt yet incapacitated by the wind... I came upon this woman the other day on 4th Street:

Now I visit her, and I don't know why ... I think she changes. I think she's changing.

December 3

The fire is a very low village tonight.

December 15

The moon is revealing the skin on its bottom. I always think of the moon, when we see it, as an homage to the sun. There is snow on the mountaintops, which gives a good feeling. Snow in the desert, though distant. There's a defunct labor/prison camp in the mountains north of Tucson. Gordon Hirabayashi was imprisoned there during the Second World War. He hitchhiked from the Northwest to the desert. When he arrived, he was sent up the mountain. Japanese-Americans, Hopi Indians, Jehovah's Witnesses, war protestors.

December 17

The clouds are starting to separate and peel off the mountains in the distance . . . There is no one here—the library is dead, and the air conditioner (installed this morning by Faulkner's widow) is loud, unnecessarily forceful. Writing is slow today. I lack the will, and want to watch movies. It feels impossible, though its a mental deficit. The plague of loss and grief, the dissolution of people . . . The impossibility of bridging regret with more than a couple of frayed ropes . . . I had a dream last night that Poppi had no legs, and moved around by way of a wheelbarrow. My mom couldn't handle it, so I had to adjust him . . . pick him up, re-wrap his bandages, make sure he was comfortable.

December 19

I have been staring at the trees. They are really something strange. I wish I could convert some molecules of what I mean into color.

December 20

I often envision very small wooden bridges to exist in the hair of old women—wooden bridges exquisitely carved, with peacock feathers. I haven't been feeling very well, and wrote fitfully all day long: wrote and read, watched the trees in the wind. It has been cloudy too, which I hate to mention for how pathetic it sounds to care, because clouds are so vital, but still.

December 20

I'm sitting between two brass candlesticks (without candles) and a vintage accordion. We're in our friends' house for the rest of the year, house-sitting, plant-watering, keeping warm . . . I just spent an hour in a wooden rocking chair in the backyard . . . The backyard is dirt and rocks, but there's a swimming pool, and young fruit trees. My back hurts. I think I'm being pressured by ghosts. Not haunted or inhabited, but pressured.

December 22

It keeps going BECAUSE it vanishes.

THE HOODED BRIDE

When the bride begins to fade...
The comet passes
...
...
Like the sun ~~goes~~ going
Underneath the world
~~You~~ The mind
Measures fluctuations
Against
A separate world   For every second, it is the human
That passes
Leaving a silent streak
...
...
With a contour
For when the ~~plan~~ earth in its endurance
Grows rabid, the final flowers
Can be sewn
Into a harness
...
To bring the body down
And let it burn
With all the number   Florid ember

Between the shoulders
...
...

...
...
The groom died, the bride
Worried for her freedom
As an object outside herself, like a new plant
...
She visited it / one visited
She had not freedom
She did not believe in God, therefore
She did not think about it
She
She
...
...
...
...
Dredged the fountain
...
Bother, Bother
The object you imagine to be the focal point
Often not, but
Shining object
In the hills

In the hill
...
The groom and the bride went walking among the dough
Found their urchin tree   barnacles and sugar crystal
Then went camping between a tan whale
And a dark green rock   The sand was soft
They stayed near the food

Bride

My fortune begins
on the
bottom of a lake
15,000 years old
...
...
scored into the land
a fossil
~~evaporated~~

I line the grave

with the pages of the book
that will succeed you →
gulf
...
jewels
...
...
a.k.a. miracle workers
to read in your
"condition changing"

Your groom
is the deafness
...

to overcome reading
...
...
awaits you
but through it
I seed my poems

wild yellow
against dark
green slopes
ascendant species
growing twds.
...
soul envisioning
...
to find it
already passed (past)
the soulless ~~indi~~
unperturbed
sober in
hybrid stables,
loving one another
as only the head-dead

the new nation
is the devil
off the ashes

I ~~sat~~ stood on a rock promontory
looking across a water cleft
at a man standing on a cliff ledge
He fell of the cliff

landed
on another   I thought he'd survive
but his body was riddled
with humors   He fell again
turning into a pinwheel
as he plummeted
toward the water   I could not see
where the sky
ground into the waves

divers can thread
the eye   at night   I mistook it
for a mouth

roots binding
with the fire
that satiates the earth
gravity enforces a sphere
…
further in

Our true audience, as
…
we diffuse
the addressee…
In letters, i.e. it's
specific
to reach the dead, we have to
diffuse the specificity
of the living →
pollinate

How do veins, I mean
snakes
get into manmade lakes?
...
Germs. Germs make snakes

empty sleeves
enjambed
where the water ends
...
...
...
black veins, birds
in the tree I mean
boomerang like
quick idea

burnt wicks on
the ends of branches
constitution
of
mature witness

Black rails, in a ragged line

Two men in a tiny boat
The melting world—sound
of distant music

smells like fish
music of a melting cage

...

...

...

the bishop of the lake
The mighty pliant (plaint)

I (thought) wanted to write to you

...

...

...

...

...

...

...

...

...

...

attuned to the impermanent (ephemeral) frequency
I might satisfy
momentarily
if I took leave of thought
as an undulating sun upon a lake
or shadow on a wall
the living operate
in blindness, preparation

It takes 50 years
for cactus to be noticed
Then the question becomes:
By whom?
And in the question
disappears

...

...

the primary description
only one needs to be seen
for an assumption to be passed
to see any other
the assumption becomes

...

~~vacuity~~ the archetype

...

maybe 100 years
the wind
the sun
companionable, relentless
to foster the alien
conductor

Then you wake
…
forgetful
the people have all been savaged
you feel neither
happy
nor remorseful

scanning the dry river
for signs
of the abject

not the margin
it runs through
…
delays

are eternal

with eyes The river is
heart

The coyote is a small tornado

                𖤐

masks are reminders

independence is
...
an event
to be mourned

People watching
me watching
the train listening

...

...

I'm not showing
anything I'm not
showing myself

following the purple's
all I remember
there were white

...

...

and insects or
the petals of
flower petals

...

...

convening
a larger purple, the most
sanitary I follow
I don't remember
the movement
when I'm in it
It is happening

...

...

...
populated again
after being depopulated
...
Movement is sagacious
The men resemble bears
and a dog
comes up to me
the littlest
sisters mother with the boys in
dog acts

hours glow
in the dark, the sound of horses in the pipes
and hungry bacteria
…
glowing
…
…
terminal

looks like
looks like
a hinge
holding together
2 mirrors

they are not sleeping
but forming tumuli

time-luxury is
...
...
one
mad heart
remaining
to turn the wall

Men go to sleep
to the respiratory moon

I asked the blind
what does "homogenous" mean

No need to justify
our days
...
to sit on
the hump
smoke eye lashes
watch the prairies come out
go back into dry sockets
...
...
stockpile,
arrange,
repudiate,
...
salvation

Haiku

The human being has expired. Long live
the human being
...
...
looks before it
leaps, it rarely leaps,
not all human beings
have made it
...
talking, sitting by
the water body,
about to compose

Outside, the trees
outside. Girl, I think,
the feeling is Girl.

Air Force
and mourning doves

As you walk
...
...
...
Your feet touch
antecedents of the world
the world has passed, but you
keep spinning
...
the water works
its way around

Dead eyes reflect
what passes before them
mirrors see
...
what is behind
a velveteen people

The hair becomes
eel grass
men line up in
August
to drink the lake

The sound was of a thousand people chewing
a thousand hooves lifting off a worn stone
a thousand windows opening (the heat from stoves)
a thousand holes cut into
the air through which
was sucked all kindness.

To try to outwit
the pervasiveness of the past
across our vantage (field
of view) is
to begin to whirl, and even more quickly, become
a screw—or
...
from another view,
a hive
around which
a colony swarms
to enter and reproduce:
the hole

pays witness
to what the hole
illuminates

Most people never
escape the hole, but make of it
a permanent home → tomb

There is a head
Hung in the willow
By the river
...
...
Hair is the willow   Warm knife by the strand
Soaked in the river   Cold ache is gone
The head eats, though a silent face
Reflects the back of the head, the
Inscrutable acre →
...
The willow sleeps with a yellow cure
...
...
Demystifies the hours [what is]
Dead in the gutter
Of the horizon, hung like
...
Marsh marigold: thick and sweating
...
...
...
Like some kind of cow
Lantern
...
Saliva

My head splits
thin lightning

gray sky without clouds
gray

to space   waves of space
...
white shores
boiling earth

Saw briefly
the silhouette of a single limb
leaves and flowers, what is it called?

HESPERIDES

Did I go outside
I walked from the market
to the apartment
to tend a memory of it
the sun, hot as brass, whomever
was out
was stale
and runny,

If someone has a voice
biology slows them down
in wanting to project
several generations

A young girl is learning to speak
In a church
Episcopal, St. Andrew's
...
...
The church is closed,
Black gate is the hair of a little head
On end. It is Monday
Only vowels coming out
...
...
Outfit and outfits
Can be recycled
To make a procession of saints
...
...
It is the second day of Holy Week
The vowels rise, each ends higher
Than where it began,
Maybe the baby's
Eyes are rolling back
She too has hair, dark brown,
Rusted green
...
...
She is standing on baked clay
Looking up into the ceiling
There is a recess set
She has not spoken yet
A day in her life

We don't speak days, we don't live
Days. They do not replenish
By our rising volumes. Andrew's head
Is blue, his heart is white, his legs
Are red. His waist is white
He looks ill, or like a boy
At the surfacing of dawn
When someone
breaks down
Everyone leans into
someone breaking
down
And touches
that one
It can go on

snails in the mouth

Evening Oracle

I looked at everyone
I wanted everyone
To be where they were

Where is it
What does it say
...
Vegetables growing in a black sash

The sun took what was
in the air
The sound of five heron
...
is when I noticed the snail eggs
...
Bright pink
Performing beforehand
...
While I stepped over the water
Where does it come?

<u>The Grave</u>
The sky might
strike you
off balance
...
...
...
And the reedy milk
of yellow hair
streaked across it
fills the ear
sends (up) the
vulnerable skin

If you see a grave on the wall,
it might mean there is a light source behind you.

The light might not be
permanent.

I thought I had finally found my place
...
...
The sparks set finally on the sill
And how the sparks grew faces

I did not know
…
I was waiting for
prefiguration

Let me sit here on this step
For a minute
I am tired
measuring personally

sparks set finally on the sill
need to be alone
need it to be late
…
…
…
…
give now each self another life?
sparks are white
with a yellow suggestion
aging
orange in the woods
…
burned off the ceremony
…
I showed up with six drinks
…

I challenged the children
to imagine that they were
on the bottom of a lake
...
sky above hundreds of feet
of glacier-cold water—
...
All the children ran first to the window
To look directly into THEIR valley
...
...
From the window glass to the mountains,
four miles in the distance

<u>sparks set finally on the sill</u>

The flattened fuses
of anarchy

You think there's hope when
Having been hopeless
Look up to see a limb
of paling green hearts
Attached by a thin flat ventricle
...
...
And where there is no water
Nor suffrage, hell-blue sky

Day draws to a
narrow close   with
faces burning
in the wash
…
first thin, then
like a fist, a flower in
the throes, then
black around
the edge, then wadded,
dead, until it fits:

Almost better not
to meet the opening on
the other side, that is
almost

The thin thread
of existence.
is real, and
is a thin thread
...
I it, but
every part is strung

When I let my vision go
what I am looking at
starts moving. It was always moving
but I lost it
in the vulgarity of my looking.

The giddiness of a map I made
the colors arranged
to meld with what I imagined
of a world to which I would've belonged
if I could have, if I had lasted

Don't burn any bridges
Daniela said
How many bridges do we need?
…
Don't go anywhere
Don't go anywhere
But into a passive perspective
service, like
…
…
people passing out with their necks open
cannot SEE the blue lights
They're negative eggs
They swallow themselves
spinsters in candles
apparatus that sparks
a bull, there are
novas being arrested

Is there really a land
with islands of grass
and yellow birds
even idiotic are affable
…
…
…
trying to unscrew
but it's okay, the bridge
will survive
the burning of the atmosphere

Day One in the
desert, I brought a book
to the park
and sat in the grass
…
ants
came out of the earth

GILA RIVER

The prisoners lived for many years—
had children   grandchildren great-grandchildren

burned   very quietly
to ash,

cut rectangles in the floor   dug holes in the dirt
to stay cool
in July   folded their bodies
like paper   fell asleep
in the holes   rivers evaporated. The prisoners disintegrated
Not even their secrets

Japanese Americans were not looking at themselves
turning white
not the cotton   not the descendants of bloodless cotton
the children's fathers refused to pick

Children were shy   had stories to tell,
not their own, but those not resolved, still dirty

a nisei woman was asked if she would like to speak, share her story
the people   facing the gleaming snow
looked sad, for a moment,   then vulturous. sad again

expectant, ready to ascend.

The nisei woman shook her head,   No, she said.
Are you sure, she was asked.
I don't remember enough
to share   She said
As she was looking through the snow   She remembered everything
but could not, seven decades later, associate herself with the subjects

When the children arrived, there were turtles Snapping turtles
like helmets   greeted the children
Turtles deep
deep deep
in the ditches, slowly rose   and snapped at the children
like Yoshiko,   wearing a dress   of her mother's crumpled face,
walked right up to the ditch
and peered in:

children were grabbed, pulled in, became turtles

How could she forget
the turtles were the solace of America

You don't forget   You are tricked,
into putting your hand in
mirror-green water. Your hand stays stuck

you stop looking

eyes were olives. Children were torches

One of each twin drowned
or burned down
to the dirt
where grandparents   on their hands and knees
re-enacted the rose, the thorn

Long hair dangled
over water   seasons stretched
camouflage nets
across the suburbs. shotgun shells   spoons, heels of shoes,
talons, forked tongues, arrow-tipped tails,
the wake of a temple
men sitting beneath spiraling flowers

mother was very popular
with the ghosts
that grew out of the ditches   they were soldiers
deep into the harmony of their hunger

Children sat on the hill
watched the desert changing colors   the stars
lower
on tendons

movies smelled   Carcasses came out

to narrate the silences

some sank into the cold, impenetrable shrapnel
fallen from tens of thousands of miles

only children remember to forget
with such warm innocence   being struck
by the sun
not innocence Guilt
not the opposite of innocence   But
like the dissolution of a flower into fruit,
compensation
and the will to be stolen

Noriyuki was eleven, had spinal TB
when he was incarcerated as an enemy of the United States   His body was cut
from the cast   and propped up
in front of the moving mirage   Noriyuki,
better
or worse known as
Mr. Miyagi, for whom Noriyuki put on the accent
of an immigrant from Okinawa

His inscrutability was part of the trick   the coming into consciousness
of a Japanese man
who had no one   war extinguished
Truth,   the country trained him
to be someone else,   not other, but native
by pretending to be someone else,   not native, but foreign

He stood in the bush
until the bush became ice

When Mr. Miyagi gets drunk   and relives the war
are we not supposed to imagine Noriyuki, the actor,
summoning the memory
of the war he was living
as a child   prisoner

is that misunderstanding
or a misunderstanding

Did you have anyone in the 442nd
No, I said,   My ancestors are not corpses
propped upright in the corner
My ancestors do not stand in cold rooms in the dark   draped with lights
round cancerous   in which my face is warped   waiting
to be turned on   dance in the window

From afar   incarceration looks like internment
It is always day
No   Japanese Americans exist
at night   The river is full   Japanese Americans gather
in the sundown   on the banks of the abundant river
to pay respects
to the primal thinking
of white men and women,   distant, futuristic
summer   or winter
or walking down the reservation

wild animals raised their heads   land stretched away
The further away from the train
the less it moved

children watched their parents' faces
framed in squares
and rectangles of light   seam of stars,
then dark,
then darkness

Did it feel like travel? guarantee of returning?
Their movements were curtailed. sound was rhythmic suture.
Dreams of the wheels slipping off

wild animals moved fast. in the shadows of rocks:

I will see you
again. incriminated
by the sadness
of someone else's dream

without ending   migration becomes internal
for those who do not leave
keep the memory leaving

de-located,

migration was a test. the destination was the extent to which
a soul could be transformed. The United States wanted to replace
with a clock,

the furnace of assimilation. earth harbors
unintelligible tongues
in the core,   tongues of flame, they are called,
the earth answers
with its cavernous body, I release you
into the custody of culture   The toll is paid
by the enslaved,
exploited, exterminated

How did it feel to be surrounded by Japanese Americans
with whom you were not related?   Prison
is prolongation   I felt like
I was standing in
a graveyard   waiting for the sun
to pass into eclipse   for the light to christen
what was buried beneath
the long, ship-like passage of shadow

I don't remember the way you remember
I don't remember a prison, but Easter
I don't remember which season or burying

In the forbidden sight
of each blackened window
a face permeated

the face of each
age of death.

fit fruitfully into
a box. Each face was made   Each face <u>made</u> real
pores that recalled
the frustrated youth of grandmothers.

Why is your skin so smooth, my grandmother asked
one night. I came out of the bathroom. I was a child.

The night was supposed to feel endless, insatiable,
was stunted   I saw myself in the window   superimposed
on a tree,   and a deer, with red eyes
cut in half

I wash my face, I said
I wash my face too

BLIND CHILDREN

When someone dies and is reborn
The fertile ground is not a force
But the will of consensus
The fertile ground cannot accommodate the reborn
Once
The reborn are living

The top half of the girl is a girl, the bottom half of the girl is a boy
Both halves come together
To complete the illusion
Children are not fractions of a single (zebra) participation
The top half of the boy is a boy, the bottom half of the boy is a girl
Two halves equal justice
In an otherwise imbalanced possession
The top half of the boy is a girl, the bottom half of the boy is a boy
Shame or not, share music or not
Books or not, bracelets or not
The top half of the girl is a boy, the bottom half of the girl is a girl
Both halves imprisoned by the gravity of halves
The sound of grapes being eaten

Two blind children are standing in a desert
Whispering to each other
Dawn. It rained last night. Did you hear the rain?
I didn't. It was very loud
I didn't hear the rain. I couldn't sleep
I didn't hear anything. I was up all night
I got up and went for a walk

Do you still love me? I don't know if I still love you
How can you not know? Because it changes
What changes? How I feel
How do you feel right now? Your head is very large
You have three necks and stubble growing down your chest
Your warts are coming off on my fingers

Black tarantulas. People sitting around a fire
Beneath enormous cottonwoods
The color of a Christian—pious, unresponsive
Faces in the smoke

The first face is the collective face
Of those who have been murdered
The second face is the face of the murderer
The classic misinterpretation: black Bolshevik beard
Decorated with small seashells
And birds resembling vaginal polyps

NONE

Friends are strangers at 11 pm
Never have I been as close
To them as
Devil to their wolves   I call them None
Are home, are in the streets
One went one way, the others another

The only way to be faithful to death, respectful to death
Is to be obscure
To death. One way. Living is (another) the many

If living becomes one, as everyone wants to live
One way, in the guise of the many
Death becomes redundant
Without faith and disrespectful

SOUL MATES

My soul mates
Have yet to be conceived

Underneath the mating
Of surrogate spirits   vacating bodies
By the minute

Directed
To live by, but I
Want to live
By the future

Ordure

I want to eat it   I want to feed it

A pool-like visage

On the crumpling horizon

Synthesized from what was being
Said or done   or done or said

And what I do

Not know

I think about

The trash

That captivates
The critical essence of soul mates

Heaven for a body that never starves

Is always starving   Drain the trash?
Fated to be

Ballast for the mass

The trash must gleam
In the middle of the desert

THE LIBRARY

Early morning: the only people in the library
Are homeless white men and Asian men
And white women who are not homeless
Asian men and women who are students
And Asian American students
And one white man and one white woman
Who are not homeless
On the 3rd floor and the 4th floor
Straightening all the chairs
The woman disappears into Anthropology
The man disappears into Education
I am in between. I am not homeless, that means sleep
I have no chairs to straighten

TOMB MODEL OF A NOBLE'S HOUSE

There are three stories, and ten visible people—four people on the first story, four people on the second story, two people on the third story; the two people on the third story, on the balcony; the four people on the second story, on the balcony; two pairs of two people, one of each pair with the arm around the other; one of the four people on the first story recessed in the shadows; the person on the far right playing the flute . . .

What are birds on the pediment?
Between the second and third stories, there is an axe
White person recessed
In the shadows   feminine people
Waiting for someone to arrive, precede death
Noble people? Projections?
Do not shine unobstructed

That something That cuts
Light penetrating indefinitely (life inside stories)
Are people   guardians (people guardians)
Patient, beatific, welcoming   there is that
Feeling   the soul
Arrives
All stories at once

Living or dead expectant (guardian facets)

Precede them? Home?
We approach
The sound of the flute
The worldly struggle to totality . . .

Are there other tombs of which this tomb
Is aware?   Like facelessness merging on balconies
Birds weaving long tails of the vagabond garment

LEUKEMIA

They painted the airplanes vibrant
Perfectly charmless colors
Then the airplanes took off
Trailing wet paint
Like a mission, the airplanes excused themselves
Into the sun, leaving the earth
A ruin of paint, long mounds of vibrant
Perfectly charmless colors
Injected with cosmetics
The people were made to drink
As the long mound seeped into
The earth, the people were bound to
An airplane? Fly in an airplane?
Excuse themselves into the sun?
All colors seeping into one
White blood

PEACH TREES

All the peaches
ORCHARD   PEACH TREES

    in the canyon   were
cut down

TEATRO

TEATRO is empty. Everyone wonders
What does TEATRO look like on the inside (inside)?
Everyone loves, but no one knows
What TEATRO looks like on the inside (inside)

Everyone loves (passes into) obscurity
Abandoned at birth

That's why everyone cries
They are born

There are no healthy or advantageous collaborations
With ones who are also alive

History left us

Stealing lemons from the neighbors' trees

Lemons are old, eating them is
Pontificating, what happened (here)? What could happen (here)?
What could we organize to make history come?
Not a face   everyone cannot get over the face, but
What touches the face is untouchable
The face is chrysalis, unknowable chrysalis

According to the whites, a situation can only be improved
By purchasing a percentage
And modifying it
Beyond the situation   the situation is always affordable
Because (According to the whites,) the whites work harder than anyone

Ancient performances were not so long ago
There was an ancient performance last night

The lights were cut
Thick dark hair was taken down
From the walls, and thrown
Into the dumpster
For the street cats

Thick dark hair justifies their standing
In the hierarchy   dogs remember

Last night's ancient performance. A young woman flew off the stage
With the entirety of her body shattered the window on the upper wall
Like the Ascension or an electrical discharge

Her body blew
A purple sky

How do we know if we are doing the right thing?
It has to be more than a momentary feeling
It has to be more than a feeling, even
There has to be something irrefutable
An example set by those who have been forsaken

Who was the young woman? No part of her remained on the stage
Yet there was something gleeful in every reference made
To the children she abandoned

They are on the market
Where garbage is thrown
Where people pass

The whites grow from where the whites
Stand admiring patterns in the smoke
Rising off the dump, demonstrable omens are
Patterns of hope (celebration)

Less auspicious, a little more embittered

Not how they see
Their loved ones all over

Legless larvae—that is why
Ghost plants, corpse plants, pipes of Indians

MOUNTAINS

There is corn growing under the highway
You can eat the corn if you are facing the mountains

Your mood will stabilize
Cars trucks and busloads of children

Sliding behind a cloud

The mountains make a very stern father, especially
When he comes out of it. He becomes playful
Forcing it—an uneasy playfulness
Ages him
Even
If necessary
To salvage something breathable

The sun goes down. The father's children stalk the shadows
He hates them, the MOUNTAINS
With a hate that does not glow
But is stately. The state is active
In feats of extraordinary landscape

DOGS

He said there's solace
Only in
Expensive matters

The kitten, maybe   Dogs can swim

When a dog barks, it means a body is passing through
Another body   the dog does not know
Which is which   the bark is broken
The penetrating body gets away

Worse if it stays

Everyone wants to
Execute the dog

When an infant pets a dog, the dog disappears
The infant becomes the bastardization of the dog
The parent is reminiscent of the infant as a bodiless rainbow
Settling in a gutter, and/or an adult
Carrying an infant into sunlight without water

We must feel for the dogs of Tucson.
Who bark as if they belong to somebody.
—Ofelia Zepeda, Proclamation

INCARCERATION

Late at night, legs in the alley
Pale blue lights
Pooling on skin   at night, legs in the alley
Attached to a navel

Every evening, the sun goes into

Money gets cold

There is a head in the willow
By the river   close to it, in it
Sucking the willow

The stain spreads

To quote the anxiety of the body
Within which memory is not

Children are asleep
On the cold cement
Sleep-like children, fish on slabs
Cold in heat, even, what is their being?
Fish on the floor, wet on the floor
Swords in a drawer

Which is your heart? Each child a mutation

Corpses in the gymnasium   bliss screwed to the ceiling

Corpses at two o'clock in the afternoon, three o'clock in the afternoon

No one home   self in a world
That is empty, bounded by time
Body is world. The world what is seen. The body unseen
Against the hard wall

Flares into a star

Hair keeps growing. Fingernails keep growing
The corpse keeps growing. The world
Does not

Other

Elements
Cannot be seen

Children cut grass, child
Out of the earth

The cage is the penultimate state
What comes after? The children dream
Carpets and coffee tables
And the little hole through which you can see someone coming
Diagonally, rabid, berserk

It is warm on this side of the little hole

Cold on that side of the little hole
Cold on this side of the little hole

When the little hole closes, the floor is cold
Everything is like a sock

The equipment is double. Teeth are dripping

Peaked with orange

The top of the head hits
The window, with spite
Is what a poet taught me one night. She was wrong
We live in the daytime is wrong

Childhood is a process, like grinding insects and flowers and rocks into pigment
With which to dodge the anemia
Or what do Americans think?

There is not enough meat? to satisfy taste?
Appetite? The king is motivated by a desire to watch children crawl
On all fours, like checkers
To the wall, the shadows
Children make
Potted cactus

One potted cactus shadow to another   they are tender
Hold silent vigils. There is a code
Communicated by breath, but only
Partly, when the body begins
To deflate
Beneath the veil
And bleed into
The drain in the middle of the floor

Blood is cold   deep-throated blood. The way dogs
Fall like shredded tires
To the dust

INCARCERATION

When I get out
I'm going to celebrate
That I was alive
Because I made myself that way
It would be easier to pick myself off
I know people did
I know people visited me in Utopia
Shared with me the meaning of death
That we return again
And again
And don't miss anything
That doesn't accomplish what
The living say about it

INCARCERATION

There seems to be no end
No matter how beautiful is

Momentary

Homogeneity

There is butter on a leaf
There is butter on the leaf I pass
Tripping like an axe

Melting, though I am momentarily less depressed

Refreshed   sitting in dried excrement
Even the attitude to quench it

For a refugee

Can seek
But when they stop, they become a prisoner
The environment does not change
A refugee must always appear to be seeking
Even after they have found what they were looking for
They pass into dream, the dream of those who came before
Prisoners of a populist order

The beginning and the end
Are interchangeable, evaporated, leaving

A landscape

Waits

But by some unexamined noise
The future of the desert
Inversion of its past

The desert
Taken away

Look at the bodies, whose existences are proof
Of the inexorable beauty
Of lives clinging tenuously

Under the weight of imminent collapse

That is

Already if

I eat the trees   will I pass the radiation?
Light green and refreshing
In the thirsty air

Through my digestive system

In which I'm barely less invasive

?

Sun is perfume   hand to hand
And never goes down

On   asylum for the mind

The sun's center is cold, always dark
The sun has not yet reached

Bodies on the slab   in razor wire
One hour until the blowflies

Are much admired
Because they think against the sun

They shine on

The Desert was written between late-2011 and late-2014 in Tucson, Arizona.

The photograph on the cover is of three Japanese Americans, taken during the Harvest Festival at the Tule Lake concentration camp, October 31, 1942. The photographer was Francis Stewart, on assignment for the War Relocation Authority. The WRA coordinated the forced removal and mass incarceration of Japanese immigrants and Japanese American citizens during WWII. Tule Lake, in northern California, was one of the ten main concentration camps. It is important to acknowledge, however, that there were, in addition to the main camps, many dozens of incarceration sites (detention centers, DOJ prisons, labor camps, segregation centers, immigration stations) stretching from Hawaii to Ellis Island, i.e. the entire United States. Tule Lake opened May 27, 1942. A segregation center opened within Tule Lake, July 15, 1943. The prison within the prison—with enhanced security, fortified fence, increased guard towers, 1000 military police—incarcerated individuals who were considered *disloyal*. Stewart took a number of photographs at Tule Lake that capture what I have written elsewhere as the *perverse psychosis that is settler colonialism in the United States* (I Am An American, *Hyperallergic*, April 1, 2017). These include photographs of Japanese Americans in blackface and children in Native American dress. (*The appearance of a young Nikkei couple in blackface in a U.S. concentration camp on land that had, until the late 1800s, been inhabited for thousands of years by the Modoc people, articulates the dynamic in which non-white people (native, alien, slave) are manipulated as the subjects and counter-subjects of a chronic performance*, I wrote.) The Harvest Festival featured performances and a parade, with hula and odori dances, kabuki, Chinese plays, minstrel shows, magic shows, clown shows. Though this photograph is in the public domain, I want to acknowledge that I first discovered it in the Densho Digital Repository, an enormously important archive of historical memory maintained by the heroic people at Densho, whose mission is *to preserve the testimonies of Japanese Americans who were unjustly incarcerated during WWII before their memories are extinguished* (densho.org, Seattle).

The epigraphs are from Malika Mokeddem's *The Forbidden Woman* (translated from the French by K. Melissa Marcus) and Mahmoud Darwish's "The Kurd Has Only The Wind" (translated from the Arabic by Fady Joudah).

[My heart is racing. First morning in Tucson.] is excerpted from emails written to Etel Adnan, Cynthia Arrieu-King, Elisabeth Benjamin, Don Mee Choi, Phil Cordelli, Dot Devota, Thom Donovan, Farnoosh Fathi, Yanara Friedland, Kate Greenstreet, Christine Shan Shan Hou, Tim Johnson, Bhanu Kapil, Youna Kwak, Quinn Latimer, Carrie Lorig, Wong May, Molly McDonald, John Melillo, Caitie Moore, Amanda Nadelberg, Kelly Schirmann, Rob Schlegel, Zachary Schomburg, Robert Yerachmiel Sniderman, Jackie Wang, Joshua Marie Wilkinson, Deborah Woodard, Lynn Xu, and Karena Youtz, from, or on the way to or from, Tucson. Thank you to my friends for their correspondence, for sharing their lives with me.

The gap in the correspondence, between May 23 and August 2, is where, during those same years, I left Tucson for Taiwan and Japan. (See: *Evening Oracle*, which, written in Japan, 2011-2012, exists inside *The Desert*, and vice versa.)

Thank you to the editors and makers of the following projects and journals, especially those who invited me to contribute: *Argos Poetry Calendar* (#5), *Capitalism Nature Socialism*, *The Carpenters & Other Strangers* (Black Cake Records), *Denver Quarterly*, *dusie* (The Asian Anglophone edition), *Elderly*, *Entropy*, *Heavy Feather Review*, *The Journal Petra*, *jubilat*, *Oversound*, *Paperbag*, *South as a State of Mind* (documenta 14), *Timber Journal*, *TYPO*.

During 2011-2014, my partner Dot Devota and I lived in many people's houses, as guests, house sitters, pet sitters, caretakers. We lived in guest rooms, casitas, backhouses, writing studios, on couches, cots. Almost all of *The Desert* was written in other people's spaces. I am grateful to everyone who shared their space, their home, with us. Thank you to the Kaohsiung American School (Kaohsiung, Taiwan), which also gave us a home, six summers in a row. Thank you to the people (friends, strangers; on Sun Tran) in the desert. Thank you to the praying mantises for their visits. Thank you to my family. Thank you to Ben Estes and Alan Felsenthal at The Song Cave.

The Desert is for Lisa

OTHER TITLES FROM THE SONG CAVE:

1. *A Dark Dreambox of Another Kind* by **Alfred Starr Hamilton**
2. *My Enemies* by **Jane Gregory**
3. *Rude Woods* by **Nate Klug**
4. *Georges Braque and Others* by **Trevor Winkfield**
5. *The Living Method* by **Sara Nicholson**
6. *Splash State* by **Todd Colby**
7. *Essay Stanzas* by **Thomas Meyer**
8. *Illustrated Games of Patience* by **Ben Estes**
9. *Dark Green* by **Emily Hunt**
10. *Honest James* by **Christian Schlegel**
11. *M* by **Hannah Brooks-Motl**
12. *What the Lyric Is* by **Sara Nicholson**
13. *The Hermit* by **Lucy Ives**
14. *The Orchid Stories* by **Kenward Elmslie**
15. *Do Not Be a Gentleman When You Say Goodnight* by **Mitch Sisskind**
16. *HAIRDO* by **Rachel B. Glaser**
17. *Motor Maids across the Continent* by **Ron Padgett**
18. *Songs for Schizoid Siblings* by **Lionel Ziprin**
19. *Professionals of Hope*, The Selected Writings of **Subcomandante Marcos**
20. *Fort Not* by **Emily Skillings**
21. *Riddles, Etc.* by **Geoffrey Hilsabeck**
22. *CHARAS: The Improbable Dome Builders*, by **Syeus Mottel** (Co-published with Pioneer Works)
23. *YEAH NO* by **Jane Gregory**
24. *Nioque of the Early-Spring* by **Francis Ponge**
25. *Smudgy and Lossy* by **John Myers**